HEAVEN

Danielle Lombardo
Illustrations by Pumudi Gardiyawasam

Dedication

~ To my Bella, who inspires me every day, may you shine God's light
and follow His path for you all the days of your life.
~ For Bella and Gabby, may you go on many God adventures
together and change the world with His love.
~ For my Bella, Gabby, Jude, Jesse, Selah, Nico, Joey, Johny, Anthony
and Chiara, may you discover all the wonderful plans that God has
in store for you and always follow His leading.
~ For all God's children, may you fully know who you are
in Christ and just how special you are to Him.

I know what I'm doing. I have it all planned out—plans to take care of you, not abandon you, plans to give you the future you hope for.

Jeremiah 29:11

Oh yes, you shaped me first inside, then out; you formed me in my mother's womb. I thank you, High God—you're breathtaking! Body and soul, I am marvelously made! I worship in adoration—what a creation! You know me inside and out, you know every bone in my body; you know exactly how I was made, bit by bit, how I was sculpted from nothing into something. Like an open book, you watched me grow from conception to birth; all the stages of my life were spread out before you, the days of my life all prepared before I'd even lived one day.

Psalm 139:13-16

On a cold winter day, Bella and Aunt Di Di were playing and telling stories, while Mommy and baby Gabriella napped.

"How do you like having a baby sister?" Aunt Di Di asked.

"She's okay, but now she's Mommy's new 'special girl,'" Bella answered.

"Oh, but you are very special! Would you like to hear a story about that?" Aunt Di Di asked.

"Yes!" Bella sang as they snuggled. "Is the story about a princess? A dragon? Or maybe a naughty turtle?"

Aunt Di Di kissed Bella's nose. "Nope! It's about a little girl sent from heaven to do a very important job."

"Wow, that sounds amazing! What's her name? She has to have a name!" Bella exclaimed.

Di Di chuckled. "Her name is Bella the Beautiful!"

"That's me, right?" Bella crinkled her nose.

"Yes, and this is your special story about how much God loves you and why He made you."

"Really?" Bella giggled. "Tell me more about how special I am."

"Before you were in Mommy's belly, God had a very special purpose for you," Aunt Di Di replied.

"Wow. He has a special porpoise for me? You mean I'm going to get a dolphin?" Bella looked at Aunt Di Di, very confused.

"Not porpoise, silly; purpose."

"Oh," Bella giggled. "What's a...purpose?"

"A purpose is a special job God created just for you," said Di Di. "Your job right now is to bring joy and love to us, but as you grow up God will show you piece by piece, like a puzzle, how you'll do your special job."

"Wow, I have a special job to do for God? That only I can do?"

"That's right, my love. He has a job that only Bella the Beautiful can do. I can't wait to see what great things He has for you."

"I can't wait either! How long do I have to wait?"

"Oh, don't worry; He will let you know in time." They hugged tightly.

"I believe that God had a little talk with you in Heaven before you were born. I can see you looking at Him in wonder and awe, just like you're looking at me now," Aunt Di Di said as she gazed into Bella's eyes.

Bella's eyes were big. "You mean I knew God in Heaven? He was my friend? What do you think He was telling me?"

"I believe that you did know Him and that He was your friend. In fact, God will always love you and be your friend no matter what!"

Then Bella jumped up and stood in her best superhero pose. "Wait! I know! I'm going to be a superhero and save the world!"

Di Di looked into Bella's eyes. "In your own way, you will save the world with His love.

"I picture God kneeling down and whispering to you, 'Bella, you are the apple of My eye! You are so beautiful, with your big eyes, cute dimples and perfectly styled hair that flips just right, but your real beauty shines through your smile and laughter and brightens people's lives.'"

"God loves me so much, right, Di Di? And I love Him sooo much, too!" Bella gave God an imaginary hug.

Aunt Di Di wiped her eyes. "Can you imagine Him hugging you back? He loves you more than you can imagine, and He never asks for anything, except for your love."

"Yes, I think I can feel Him hugging me back, Di Di! It feels like my daddy hugging me! I feel the love!"

Aunt Di Di tenderly kissed Bella. "From the moment you were born, you've added so much to our lives. God sent you to our family at the perfect time! You've brought more love and joy than we could've ever imagined."

"You mean like when we sing, 'You make my heart so happy?' Is that the joy you mean?" Aunt Di Di laughed in agreement as she and Bella danced and sang their special song together.

"Yes, that is just a little piece of it," Aunt Di Di said as they collapsed in a hug.

"I love you this much, Aunt Di Di," Bella said with her arms wide open.

"And I love you to the moon and back, sweetheart!" Aunt Di Di replied.

"I can just imagine how, before He sent you to us, He said, 'My beautiful daughter, I know the perfect family for you. They will love you, and you will remind them of My love for them.' That, my sweet Bella, is your purpose: to be a reminder of God's love for us," Aunt Di Di explained.

"But how?"

"You do it already! You give hugs and kisses. You say funny things that make us laugh. You do it just by being you."

"Wow! I can do that!" Bella jumped with joy. "Being me is easy!"

"Just watching you grow and seeing all the new things you do brings us excitement and joy. Our heavenly Father celebrates with us as He watches over you."

"Does He see my mess-ups, too?" Bella asked.

"Yes, He sees everything, but that's why He sent His Son, Jesus, to pick you up again," answered Aunt Di Di.

"So, Jesus helps me fix my mess-ups and try again?" Bella asked thoughtfully.

"Yes, exactly! He will always be there to help you. All you have to do is ask," Aunt Di Di answered lovingly.

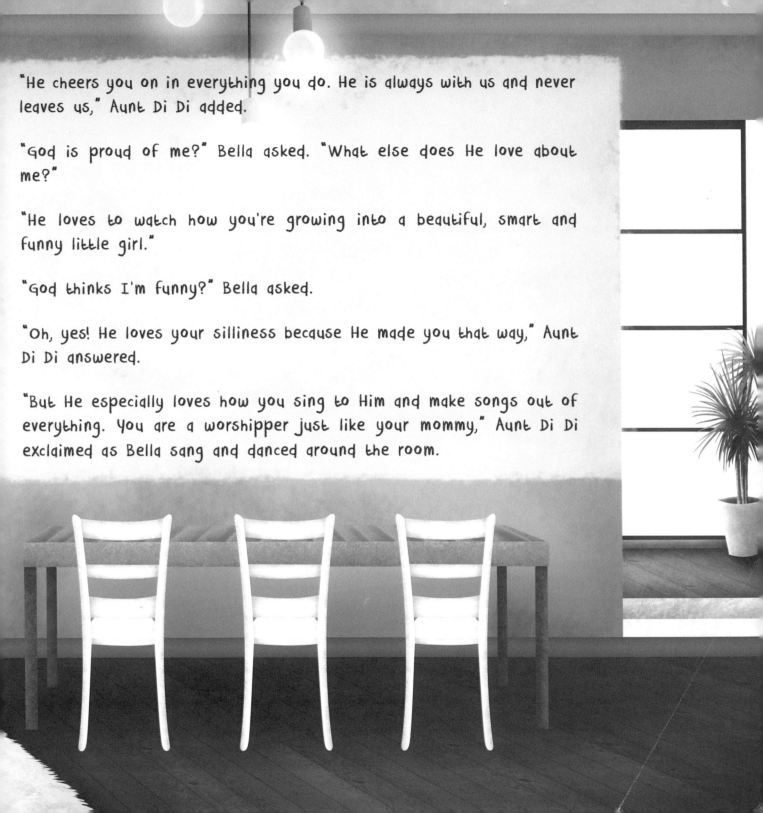

"He cheers you on in everything you do. He is always with us and never leaves us," Aunt Di Di added.

"God is proud of me?" Bella asked. "What else does He love about me?"

"He loves to watch how you're growing into a beautiful, smart and funny little girl."

"God thinks I'm funny?" Bella asked.

"Oh, yes! He loves your silliness because He made you that way," Aunt Di Di answered.

"But He especially loves how you sing to Him and make songs out of everything. You are a worshipper just like your mommy," Aunt Di Di exclaimed as Bella sang and danced around the room.

"Does He love it when I pray?" Bella asked.

"He sure does! He loves how you pray for our boo-boos or when we don't feel well, and your sweet 'Amen' after every prayer warms His heart," Aunt Di Di said.

"I love it, too," said Bella. "I love to pray for everyone, just like they pray for me when I feel sick."

"He loves your simple faith. It's the kind of faith God wants us all to have," Aunt Di Di replied.

Aunt Di Di exclaimed, "God is sooo proud of you, Bella, and so am I."

"Wow, really! That makes me so happy," Bella sang, jumping up and down. "I want to make Him proud of me forever!"

"He is and always will be! Just imagine how proud we are of you, but a million times more," Aunt Di Di said with arms wide open.

"God wants us to know how much He loves us so we can show His love to others and change the world," Aunt Di Di said. "Every time you sing a song to Him or do something that shows His love, there's a party in heaven!"

"God hears my songs and has parties in heaven with His angels because of me?" Bella asked.

"Yes! Heaven's parties are more beautiful than you can imagine! In fact, they don't even need decorations. Most of all, He loves your sweet songs," Aunt Di Di replied.

"Oh, wow!" Bella's eyes grew dreamy as she imagined what heaven's parties are like. "Then I'll sing more songs for Him if He loves them that much."

"He would love that," said Di Di.

"But wait!" Aunt Di Di exclaimed. "God just gave you another important piece of your purpose. You have a brand-new baby sister. You're a big sister! How exciting!" Aunt Di Di said joyfully.

"But how is being a big sister a part of my purpose?" Bella asked.

"Well, your job is to teach Gabriella how much God loves her and how special He made her. You both have special purposes," Aunt Di Di replied.

"Okay!" Bella exclaimed. "I'll teach her how special she is!"

"I know you will," Aunt Di Di said. "You'll have many wonderful adventures as you grow up together."

"I love her so much and can't wait to have fun with her." Bella ran to hug her baby sister as her mommy entered with Gabriella in her arms.

"She loves you, too." Aunt Di Di hugged Bella as she prayed:

"My prayer is that you and your sister will always be best friends, just like your mommy and I are. I pray that you will always feel God's love and joy over you as you grow and that you both follow the paths God has for you. And last, but not least, I pray that you always remember you were 'heaven sent'. I pray this in Jesus' name. Amen."

"Amen!" exclaimed Bella.

ISBN 978-1-945169-52-6

Published by
Little Blessing Books
an imprint of
Orison Publishers, Inc.
www.OrisonPublishers.com

CPSIA information can be obtained
at www.ICGtesting.com
Printed in the USA
BVRC100402210521
607812BV00016B/2